Echalon Maps

EUROPE

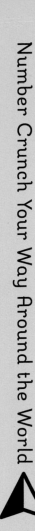

Joanne Randolph

Raintree is an imprint of Capstone Global Library
Limited, a company incorporated in England and Wales
having its registered office at 264 Banbury Road, Oxford
OX2 7DY – Registered company number: 6695582

www.raintree.co.uk
myorders@raintree.co.uk

Text © Capstone Global Library Limited 2016
The moral rights of the proprietor have been asserted.

Produced for Raintree by Calcium
Edited by Sarah Eason and Katie Woolley
Designed by Paul Myerscough
Illustrations by Moloko88/Shutterstock
Picture research by Sarah Eason
Production by Victoria Fitzgerald
Originated by Capstone Global Library Ltd © 2016
Printed and bound in China

ISBN 978 1 4747 1595 9 (hardback)
19 18 17 16 15
10 9 8 7 6 5 4 3 2 1

ISBN 978 1 4747 1601 7 (paperback)
20 19 18 17 16
10 9 8 7 6 5 4 3 2 1

British Library Cataloguing in Publication Data
A full catalogue record for this book is available from the
British Library.

Acknowledgements
We would like to thank the following for permission
to reproduce photographs: Shutterstock: A.B.G. 16,
29b, Atm2003 6bl, Ivan Bastien 14tr, Greg Blok 26t,
Aleksander Bolbot 24l, Burben 5t, Canadastock 6r, 11c,
28l, 29t, Bucchi Francesco 26b, Filip Fuxa 18t, Giedriius
7t, Goodcat 12l, Dave Head 21r, Patricia Hofmeester 19tl,
JuliaLine 9r, Iakov Kalinin 4br, Kekyalyaynen 7r, Alan Kraft
23tl, Philip Lange 4bl, Littleny 20r, 28r, Viacheslav Lopatin
27r, Oleksiy Mark 17tr, Martin M303 18bl, MilousSK 25r,
Jaroslav Moravcik 24br, Andrei Nekrassov 14b, Gardar
Olafsson 19b, Inacio Pires 13tl, Andrei Pop 15r, Nicram
Sabod 16tr, SF photo 11br, Sergey Sizov 10tr, Stocker1970
20tr, 26l, Stockphoto-graf 1, 12r, TTstudio 5b, Maria
Uspenskaya 13br, Vaclav Volrab 9bl, XXLPhoto 22l;
Wikimedia Commons: Koosha Paridel 23r, Stefg74 8tr.

Cover photographs reproduced with permission of:
Dreamstime: Ryhor Bruyeu (top), Zoom-zoom (bottom);
Shutterstock: Ivan Bastien (back cover).

Some words are shown in bold, **like this**. You can
find out what they mean by looking in the glossary.

Contents

Europe

Europe is the birthplace of western **culture**. Europeans have influenced every **continent**, through exploration and sometimes **colonization**, from the 1500s through to the 1900s. Europeans colonized the Americas, Africa, Australia and much of Asia. Are you ready to explore this region using your best map and maths skills?

How to use this book

Look for the "Map-a-stat" and "Do the maths" features and complete the maths challenges. Then look at the answers on pages 28 and 29 to see if your calculations are correct.

A lot of peninsulas

Europe is a **peninsula**. This means that it is surrounded by water on three sides. The interesting thing about Europe is that its peninsula is made up of many smaller peninsulas. Some of the larger ones are the Iberian, Italian, Balkan, Jutland and Scandinavian peninsulas.

North Sea

Atlantic Ocean

Strait of Gibraltar

Venice, Italy

The Northern Lights can be seen in some northern regions of Europe.

Map-a-stat

The Iberian Peninsula is the third-largest European peninsula. It has an area of around 582,750 sq km (225,000 sq miles). It is made up of Portugal, Andorra, Spain, part of France and the Gibraltar territory.

The Italian Peninsula is sometimes called the "boot" for its shape. The peninsula stretches for around 960 km (600 miles) from north to south.

The Balkan Peninsula includes a number of countries, such as Albania, Bosnia & Herzegovina, Bulgaria, Croatia, Macedonia, Montenegro, Romania, Serbia, Slovenia and Moldova. It has a total area of around 666,700 sq km (257,400 sq miles).

Black Sea

Mediterranean Sea

DO THE MATHS!

Use the information in red in the Map-a-stat box to work out the following challenge. How long would it take you to drive from the Po Valley at the north of the Italian Peninsula to the Mediterranean Sea in the south, if you drove at a rate of 80 km per hour? Here is the equation to help you solve the problem.

$$960 \text{ km} \div 80 \text{ km per hour} = ? \text{ hours}$$

Complete the maths challenge, then turn to pages 28—29 to see if your calculation is correct!

Prague, Czech Republic

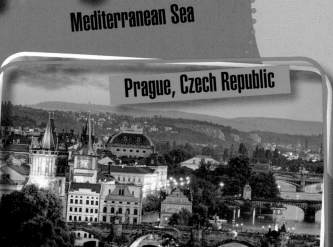

What a continent!

Europe is the world's second-smallest continent by size. It is 9.93 million sq km (3.83 million sq miles) in area. It is the third-largest continent by population, which is around 742 million.

So many habitats

Europe has many different **ecosystems** and **habitats** for its plants and animals. It has **tundra** and **taiga** in the far north, and forests, **grasslands** and **pasturelands** in western and central Europe. The regions along the Mediterranean Sea have a mild **climate** and crops such as olives and grapes are grown there.

The land around the Alps is covered in forests and grasslands.

Tuscany, in Italy, has many protected natural areas.

Map-a-stat

Around 25 per cent of the animal species in Europe are endangered. Some of this is caused by habitat loss, pollution or hunting by people. Some is caused by competition from other species not typically from the area.

Asia and Africa both have more people than Europe. Asia's population is around 4.4 billion and Africa's population is around 1.1 billion.

There are 50 widely recognized countries in Europe.

Asia and Africa both

This hare lives in the Scottish Highlands.

DO THE MATHS!

Use the information in red in the Map-a-stat box to work out the following challenge. The population of the world is around 7 billion. If you add the populations of the two most populated continents, Africa and Asia, how many people live in the rest of the world? Here is the equation to help you solve the problem.

$$7,000,000,000 \text{ people} - (4,400,000,000 + 1,100,000,000 \text{ people}) = ? \text{ people in the rest of the world}$$

Karelia, an area found in both Finland and Russia, has the two largest lakes in Europe.

Complete the maths challenge, then turn to pages 28—29 to see if your calculation is correct!

Mountains

Europe has many beautiful mountain ranges. The Alps are in the southern part of central Europe and run for 1,207 km (750 miles). They are known for their amazing views, lakes, valleys and glaciers, and they offer some of the best skiing in the world. The Balkan Mountains run from Bulgaria to the Black Sea. The highest peak in Greece is Mount Olympus. It was home to the gods of Greek myths. Other mountain ranges include the Carpathians, the Caucasus, the Pyrenees, the Apennines and the Urals.

Mount Narodnaya

Urals

Carpathians

Caucasus

Matterhorn   Alps

Mont Blanc

Pyrenees

Mount Elbrus

Apennines

Mount Olympus

Balkans

The Ural Mountains

The Ural Mountains form the natural border between Asia and Europe. They run from the northern edge of the Russian Federation in Europe, through Kazakhstan. They are around 2,500 km (1,550 miles) long.

Map-a-stat

The highest point in the Alps is Mont Blanc at 4,807 m (15,771 ft).

The highest point in the Ural Mountains is Mount Narodnaya at 1,895 m (6,217 ft).

Mount Olympus is 2,916 m (9,568 ft).

Mount Elbrus is considered by many people to be the highest peak in Europe.

Mytikas is the highest of Mount Olympus's 52 peaks.

The Matterhorn is a peak in the Alps.

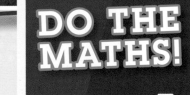

DO THE MATHS!

Use the information in red in the Map-a-stat box to work out the following challenge. How much higher is Mont Blanc than Mount Narodnaya? Here is the equation to help you solve the problem.

$$4,807 \text{ m} - 1,895 \text{ m} = ? \text{ m higher}$$

Complete the maths challenge, then turn to pages 28—29 to see if your calculation is correct!

Rivers

Hundreds of rivers and their smaller branches, called **tributaries**, flow through the European continent to the sea. The Danube is one of the longest rivers in Europe. It flows 2,850 km (1,771 miles) from the Black Forest in Germany to empty into the Black Sea. The Dnieper and the Don Rivers both begin in the Russian Federation, part of which is also found in Asia. The Elbe starts in the Czech Republic and flows north into the North Sea.

Volga River

Rhine River

Elbe River

Don River

Dnieper River

Loire River

Po River

Danube River

The Rhine and the Danube

The Rhine and the Danube are famous for once forming the border of the Roman Empire. The Rhine is considered to flow between 1,232–1,319 km (766–820 miles) from the Swiss Alps and empties into the North Sea. The Rhine River's course is shorter today than it once was, though. The course was changed to accommodate a number of **canals** that improved its use as a waterway.

Map-a-stat

The Po River, at 652 km (405 miles) long, is the longest river in Italy.

The Loire River is the longest river in France. It flows 1,020 km (634 miles) from southern France into the Bay of Biscay in the northwest.

The Danube River passes Aggstein Castle in Austria.

At Nizhny Novgorod the Volga River is joined by the Oka River.

DO THE MATHS!

Use the information in red in the Map-a-stat box to work out the following challenge. If you travel at a rate of 8 km per hour, how long would it take you to travel down the entire length of the Po River? Here is the equation to help you solve the problem.

$$652 \text{ km} \div 8 \text{ km per hour} = ? \text{ hours}$$

Complete the maths challenge, then turn to pages 28—29 to see if your calculation is correct!

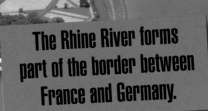

The Rhine River forms part of the border between France and Germany.

The Mediterranean Basin

The Mediterranean Basin covers parts of Europe, Asia and Africa. This region refers to the lands around the Mediterranean Sea. They have mild, rainy winters and hot, dry summers. Europe's Mediterranean Basin includes parts of the countries of France, Italy, Greece, Croatia, Spain, Albania and others.

Venice, Italy, is part of the Mediterranean Basin.

Goats live happily along the rocky coasts of the Mediterranean Basin.

Mediterranean plants and animals

Countries around the Mediterranean have **scrublands, savannas**, woodlands and some forests, especially at high ground. They are known for growing olive trees, citrus fruits, figs, cork oak and herbs such as rosemary, thyme, sage and oregano. Animals such as wild goats, sheep, cattle, **lynx** and rabbits are just a few of the creatures that live there. The climate also provides good **grazing** land for **livestock.**

Map-a-stat

Cork oak trees can live for up to 250 years. They are the source for cork used to make many items, including cork boards, wine corks and flooring. Around 299,000 tonnes (330,000 tons) of cork are harvested in the western Mediterranean Basin each year, and 66 per cent is made into bottle stoppers.

The Barbary macaque, a kind of monkey, lives in the Mediterranean region. In Europe, it lives in Gibraltar. There are around 230 animals living there in five troops, or groups.

The Mediterranean Basin, which includes land in Africa and Asia, has an area of around 2,098,000 sq km (810,000 sq miles).

These cork trees have been stripped of their bark, which will be used to make cork products.

DO THE MATHS!

Use the information in red in the Map-a-stat box to work out the following challenge. What percentage of cork harvested in the western Mediterranean is used to make things other than bottle stoppers? Here is the equation to help you solve the problem.

$$100 \text{ per cent} - 66 \text{ per cent} = ? \text{ per cent}$$

Complete the maths challenge, then turn to pages 28—29 to see if your calculation is correct!

Vineyards such as this one are common in the Mediterranean region.

Greece

Greece is a country in southern Europe. It is also known as the Hellenic Republic, and has a population of around 11 million people. Greece is at a crossroads between Europe, Asia and Africa. It is known for its many beautiful islands. It has more than 2,000 islands but only 170 have people living on them.

Greek geography

Greece has many mountains. Around 80 per cent of its land is covered in hills and mountains. The country also has the second-longest coastline in Europe, at 13,676 km (8,498 miles).

Bulgaria

Turkey

Macedonia

Albania

Greece

Athens

Crete

Mediterranean Sea

Crete is Greece's largest island.

Map-a-stat

The island of Crete has a population of 623,000. Euboea, the second-largest Greek island, has a population of about 207,000.

Athens is Greece's capital It is also one of the world's oldest cities.

The city alone has a population of 664,000. The population, including the city of Athens and the surrounding urban area, is more than 3 million people.

The Parthenon sits atop the Acropolis in Athens, Greece.

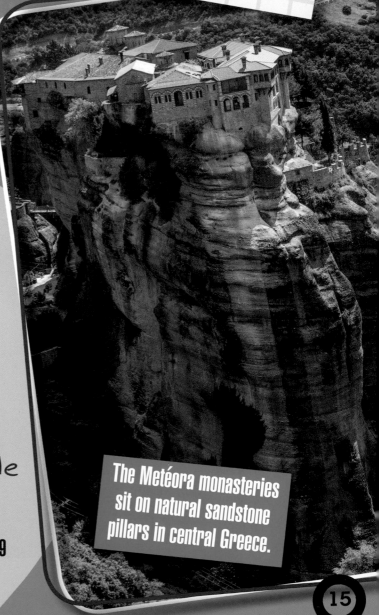

The Metéora monasteries sit on natural sandstone pillars in central Greece.

DO THE MATHS!

Use the information in red in the Map-a-stat box to work out the following challenge. How many more people live on Crete than on Euboea? Here is the equation to help you solve the problem.

623,000 people − 207,000 people = ? more people

Complete the maths challenge, then turn to pages 28—29 to see if your calculation is correct!

The Nordic countries

The **Nordic countries** are the nations in the northern part of the European continent. They are Denmark, Finland, Iceland, Norway and Sweden. There are also a few territories in the Atlantic Ocean, including Greenland.

Norway is known for its fjords, which are deep inlets of sea bordered by steep hills or cliffs.

Land of glaciers and ice caps

With an area of around 3.4 million sq km (1.3 million sq miles), if the Nordic countries were one country it would be the seventh-largest country in the world. More than 50 per cent of the land there has no people living on it. These areas are extremely cold and are covered in **ice caps** and glaciers. However, below the **Arctic Circle**, much of the Nordic coast has a mild climate. This is because the Norwegian Current brings warm waters to the coast.

Norwegian Sea

Iceland

Sweden

Norway

Finland

Atlantic Ocean

North Sea

Denmark

Map-a-stat

Even if you do not include Greenland, the Faroe Islands and the Norwegian archipelagos of Svalbard and Jan Mayen, the area of the Nordic countries is still huge. It covers 1,258,336 sq km (485,846 sq miles). That is almost as big as France, Germany and Italy combined, which have a total area of 1,302,163 sq km (502,767 sq miles).

The Sami are the native people of the Arctic area of Sápmi, also known as Laplar. This is made up of northern Norway, Sweden, Finland and the Kola Peninsula of Russia. The Sami's homelands have an area of around 388,500 sq km (150,000 sq miles).

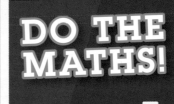
Stockholm is the capital of Sweden.

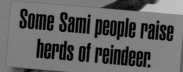
Some Sami people raise herds of reindeer.

DO THE MATHS!

Use the information in red in the Map-a-stat box to work out the following challenge. How many more square km is the total area of France, Germany and Italy than the total area of the Nordic countries? Here is the equation to help you solve the problem.

$$1,302,163 \text{ sq km}$$
$$- 1,258,336 \text{ sq km}$$
$$= ? \text{ sq km}$$

Complete the maths challenge, then turn to pages 28–29 to see if your calculation is correct!

Iceland

Iceland is one of the Nordic countries. It is an island that has an area of around 103,000 sq km (40,000 sq miles). The island has only a small population, with just 326,300 people living there.

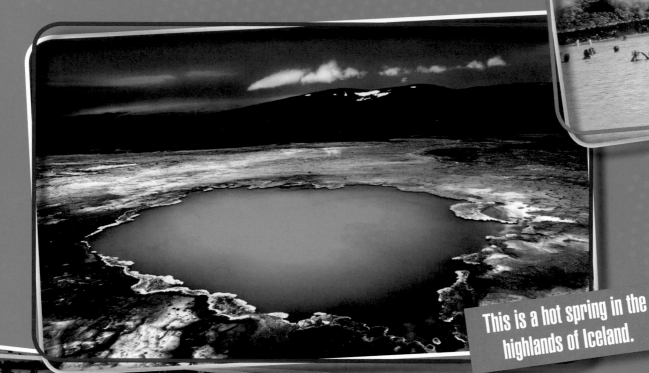

This is a hot spring in the highlands of Iceland.

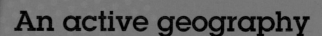

Reykjavík is the capital of Iceland.

An active geography

Iceland sits on the mid-Atlantic ridge, which is between two tectonic plates in Earth's surface. The island has many active volcanoes and geysers. All this underground activity has its uses. Tourists and locals visit the many hot springs in Iceland. The steam from the hot springs is used to generate electricity, and the country's underground heat is used for heating and hot water.

Map-a-stat

About 61 per cent of Iceland's people live in and around Reykjavék.

Strokkur is a geyser in Iceland that erupts every 5 to 10 minutes.

About 85 per cent of Iceland's energy comes from renewable energy sources (energy that will not run out), such as geothermal power.

The hot springs at Grindavík, Iceland, are a popular attraction.

Smoke and ash erupt from an Icelandic volcano.

DO THE MATHS!

Use the information in red in the Map-a-stat box to work out the following challenge. How many times does Strokkur erupt in one hour? Here are the equations to help you solve the problem.

60 minutes ÷ 10 minutes = ? times per hour

60 minutes ÷ 5 minutes = ? times per hour

So it erupts between ? and ? times per hour

Complete the maths challenge, then turn to pages 28—29 to see if your calculation is correct!

The British Isles

The British Isles are made up of the two islands of Great Britain and Ireland, and more than 5,000 smaller islands, including the Isle of Man, the Hebrides and the Shetland Islands. The British Isles are in northwestern Europe and their western border is the Atlantic Ocean. They are also bordered by the North Sea, the Irish Sea and the English Channel. Great Britain is made up of three countries: England, Scotland and Wales. The United Kingdom includes Great Britain as well as Northern Ireland.

Shetland Islands

Hebrides

Dublin is Ireland's capital and largest city.

Orkney Islands

Loch Morar

Scotland

Northern Ireland

Isle of Man

Lough Neagh

England

River Severn

Ireland

River Shannon

Wales

River Thames

Bodies of water

The largest lake in the British Isles by area is Lough Neagh in Northern Ireland. It has an area of 391 sq km (151 sq miles). Some of the other main lakes are Loch Lomond, Loch Ness and Loch Morar, which is the deepest lake in the region. The longest river is the River Shannon in Ireland, which runs 372 km (231 miles). Great Britain's longest river is the River Severn.

Map-a-stat

The British Isles has more than 5,000 islands, but only about 136 of these islands have people living on them.

Great Britain has an area of 209,331 sq km (80,823 sq miles). Ireland has an area of 84,421 sq km (32,595 sq miles). The total area of the British Isles is around 315,130 sq km (121,670 sq miles).

The United Kingdom has 14 overseas territories, though some of these are disputed, which means not everyone agrees on who controls them.

Ben Nevis, in Scotland, is the highest point in the British Isles, at 1,343 m (4,406 ft).

Arlington Row is a row of medieval cottages in the village of Bibury, England.

Hadrian's Wall separated England from Scotland in Roman times.

DO THE MATHS!

Use the information in red in the Map-a-stat box to work out the following challenge. How much of the area of the British Isles is not taken up by Great Britain and Ireland? Here is the equation to help you solve the problem.

$$315,130 \text{ sq km} - (209,331 + 84,421 \text{ sq km}) = ? \text{ sq km}$$

Complete the maths challenge, then turn to pages 28–29 to see if your calculation is correct!

The Straits

There are many straits in Europe. Straits are narrow waterways that connect two large areas of water, such as seas. One of these straits is the **Strait of Otranto**, which separates Italy from Albania and connects the Ionian Sea with the Adriatic Sea. The **Strait of Gibraltar** separates Africa from Spain. It is just 13 km (8 miles) wide at its narrowest point.

Dover Strait

Øresund⊠

Bosphorus

Strait of Gibraltar

Strait of Otranto

the chalk cliffs along the Strait of Dover

Strait of Dover

The Strait of Dover separates Great Britain from France. The strait is at the narrowest part of the English Channel. The strait is famous as being a favourite crossing point for swimmers trying to swim the Channel. It is also famous for the white chalk cliffs along the coast.

the Strait of Gibraltar

Map-a-stat

The Strait of Gibraltar is between 298-899 m (980-2,950 ft.) deep. Many ferries cross the waterway each day. It takes each ferry about 35 minutes to cross the strait.

The Strait of Dover is about 33 km (21 miles) wide at its narrowest point.

At its narrowest point, the Strait of Otranto is less than 72 km (45 miles) across.

The Bosphorus Strait forms part of the boundary between Europe and Asia.

DO THE MATHS!

Use the information in red in the Map-a-stat box to work out the following challenge. How long would it take a swimmer to cross the narrowest section of the English Channel, swimming at a rate of 3.2 km per hour and assuming all conditions were good? Here is the equation to help you solve the problem.

$$33 \text{ km} \div 3.2 \text{ km per hour} = ? \text{ hours}$$

Complete the maths challenge, then turn to pages 28—29 to see if your calculation is correct!

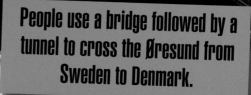

People use a bridge followed by a tunnel to cross the Øresund from Sweden to Denmark.

The European Plain

The European Plain is a large plain. It stretches from the Pyrenees Mountains and the French coast in the west to the Ural Mountains in the east. It has a mostly **temperate** climate, with farmland and forests, but it also has areas of **steppe** or dry grassland. Most of the plain is less than 152 m (500 ft.) above sea level.

North European Plain

Human settlement

People tend to live where there are a lot of resources, and access to water, good farmland and **trade routes**. In many cases, these kinds of places are found along coasts. However, because the European Plain has so many rivers running through it, it is one of the most highly populated regions in Europe.

Bialowieza Forest

Sheep graze on the European Plain's grasslands.

East European Plain

Bialowieza Forest

Map-a-stat

The European Plain is split into two parts, the East European Plain and the North European Plain. The eastern plain is the larger part and has an area of around 4 million sq km (1.5 million sq miles).

In the west, the plain is narrow, at around 321 km (200 miles) across, but it widens to more than 3,218 km (2,000 miles) in the east near the mountains.

The European Plain is home to a very old forest that has been largely undisturbed since ancient times. It is called the Bialowieza Forest. It is home to 800 bison, which are Europe's largest animals.

DO THE MATHS!

Use the information in red in the Map-a-stat box to work out the following challenge. How long would it take you to hike across the narrowest part of the European Plain, walking at a rate of 6 km per hour? Here is the equation to help you solve the problem.

$$321 \text{ km} \div 6 \text{ km per hour} = ? \text{ hours}$$

Complete the maths challenge, then turn to pages 28—29 to see if your calculation is correct!

European bison

An amazing continent

Europe is an amazing continent, with Arctic tundra, mountains, beautiful forests and plenty of beaches along its coasts. It also has many wonderful cities, such as **Prague** in the **Czech Republic** and **Dublin** in **Ireland**, that mix their long history with modern culture. Tourists from around the world visit Europe to see its countryside and to explore the architecture, art and culture of its many cities.

Madrid is Spain's capital.

London

Paris

Dublin

Prague

Madrid

Rome

The Eiffel Tower is a symbol of Paris, France.

London is the UK capital.

Wonderful cities

Some of the most famous and visited of Europe's cities are London, Paris and Rome. London, the capital of the United Kingdom, has a history that is almost 2,000 years old. Today, London is a busy city and one of the leading financial centres of the world. Paris is the capital of France. The city's metropolitan area has a population of around 10 million people. It is known for its beautiful buildings and excellent food. Rome, the capital of Italy, is a modern city with an ancient history. Many ancient ruins, such as the Colosseum, are reminders of ancient Roman civilization. The city has architecture from many other eras in history, as well.

Map-a-stat

London's metropolitan area has a population of 8.3 million people.

Paris has an area of around 105 sq km (40 sq miles), though the city's metropolitan area is about

17,069 sq km (6,590 sq miles) larger than the city.

It is thought that the Colosseum, a stadium built in Rome around AD 70, could hold 50,000 people.

DO THE MATHS!

Use the information in red in the Map-a-stat box to work out the following challenge. What is the size of Paris's city and metropolitan area combined? Here is the equation to help you solve the problem.

105 sq km
+ 17,069 sq km
= ? sq km

Complete the maths challenge, then turn to pages 28—29 to see if your calculation is correct!

the Colosseum, Rome

Maths challenge answers

You have made it through the mathalon! How did your maths skills measure up? Check your answers below.

Page 5

960 km ÷ 80 km per hour = 12 hours

DO THE MATHS!

Page 7

7,000,000,000 people – (4,400,000,000 + 1,100,000,000 people) = 1,500,000,000 people in the rest of the world

Page 9

4,807 m – 1,895 m = 2,912 m higher

Page 11

652 km ÷ 8 km per hour = 81.5 hours

Page 13

100 per cent – 66 per cent = 34 per cent

Page 15

623,000 people – 207,000 people
= 416,000 more people

Page 17

1,302,163 sq km – 1,258,336 sq km
= 43,827 sq km

Page 19

60 minutes ÷ 10 minutes = 6 times per hour
60 minutes ÷ 5 minutes = 12 times per hour
so it erupts between 6 and 12 times per hour

Page 21

315,130 sq km –
(209,331 + 84,421 sq km)
= 21,378 sq km

Page 23

33 km ÷ 3.2 km per hour = 10.3 hours

Page 25

321 km ÷ 6 km
per hour = 53.5 hours

Page 27

105 sq km
+ 17,069 sq km
= 17,174 sq km

Glossary

archipelago group of islands

Arctic Circle imaginary line encircling the northernmost areas of the Earth

bison large wild mammal, similar to an ox

canal man-made waterway

climate kind of weather a certain area has

colonization settling of new land and the claiming of it for the government of another country

continent one of Earth's seven large landmasses

culture beliefs, practices and arts of a group of people

ecosystem community of living things and the surroundings in which they live

endangered describing a species that is in danger of dying out

geothermal power power created by using steam from Earth's underground heat

geyser hot spring that sometimes shoots out jets of hot water or steam

glacier large mass of ice that moves down a mountain or along a valley

grassland large area of land covered by grass

grazing eating grass

habitat surrounding area in which plants and animals naturally live

ice cap large, thick sheet of ice covering an area of land

livestock farm animal reared by humans

lynx type of large, short-tailed wild cat

metropolitan area very large, heavily populated urban area, including all of its suburbs

myth story passed down in a particular culture. Many myths explain how the world began and why it is the way it is.

pastureland grassland used by animals for grazing

peninsula area of land surrounded by water on three sides

savanna area of grassland with few trees or bushes

scrubland area of low trees and bushes

species single kind of living thing. All people are one species.

steppe area of dry, open grassland

strait narrow waterway that connects two larger bodies of water

taiga forest with fir, spruce or other types of trees with cones and needle-like leaves. Taiga often starts where the frozen tundra ends.

tectonic plate moving pieces of Earth's crust, the top layer of Earth

temperate not too hot or too cold

territory a particular area of land that belongs to and is controlled by a country

trade route route along which people buy and sell goods

tributary small river or stream that flows into a larger river

tundra cold, treeless plain with permanently frozen soil

volcano opening in Earth's crust through which ash, gases and melted rock are forced out

Find out more

Books

Adventures Around the Globe, Lonely Planet Kids
(Lonely Planet, 2015)

Europe (Countries in Our World), Galya Ransome
(Franklin Watts, 2012)

Europe: Everything You Ever Wanted to Know (Not for Parents)
(Lonely Planet, 2014)

Introducing Europe (Introducing Continents), Chris Oxlade
and Anita Ganeri (Raintree, 2013)

Websites

There is a lot to learn about Europe's geography at:
**education.nationalgeographic.com/education/
encyclopedia/europe-physical-geography/?ar_a=1**

Find out about all the different countries in Europe at:
www.ducksters.com/geography/europe.php

Find out a lot of amazing facts about Europe at:
www.worldatlas.com/webimage/countrys/eu.htm

Index